Snow Leopards

Hunters of the Snow and Ice

Elaine Landau

ANIMALS of the SNOW and ICE

Contents

Words to Know

endangered—A kind of animal that is in danger of disappearing from Earth forever.

habitat—The place where an animal or plant lives.

marmot—A small furry animal found in high mountain areas.

prey—An animal that is hunted by another animal for food.

stalk—To hunt an animal in a quiet, secret way.

An Animal of the Snow and Ice

You are climbing a high mountain in Tibet, a country in Asia. It has been snowing and the cold wind sends chills through you. You look down and see paw prints in the white snow.

A large, beautiful animal stands in the distance. It is a big cat with a strong, muscular body. You watch it move gracefully down the side of the mountain.

You know how lucky you are. This big cat is very rare. Few people have ever seen it in the wild. It is found in only a few cold, high mountain areas. You have just spotted a snow leopard.

Snow leopards live in the areas on this map that are marked in orange.

What a Cat!

Snow leopards do not look like other leopards. They have mostly long, thick, off-white fur. Their coats are dotted with dark spots.

These cats also are slightly smaller than other leopards. They are about two feet tall at the shoulder. Their bodies are between three and four feet long. That is about the length of a third-grader lying down.

Snow leopards weigh between sixty and one hundred twenty pounds. The average adult male weighs about one hundred pounds, which is as much as twelve average house cats.

These beautiful big cats have really long tails. Their tails are about three feet long—nearly as long as their bodies!

Getting Around

Snow leopards are very graceful. They move quickly and quietly. Their wide feet work like snowshoes. They spread the large cat's weight over a broad area so that the animal can walk on top of the snow without sinking into it. Their feet's padding protects them from sharp rocks.

These big cats are also good runners. They can run very fast for short distances. They are great at climbing and leaping, too. They can leap as far as thirty feet—the length of a school bus. No human can come close to doing that. Not many other animals can, either!

Snow leopards can jump about the length of a school bus!

Home Sweet Home

Snow leopards are mountain animals. They do not live in groups. Much of their time is spent alone. These big cats are found in the snow-covered mountain areas of Central Asia. More than half of them may live in China.

Snow leopards live high in the mountains where winter is cold and windy. They are at home in steep, rocky places. They have been spotted on cliffs and ridges.

In the winter many animals move further down the mountain, including the wild sheep and goats. They are looking for food to eat. Snow leopards move down the mountain then, too. These big cats are meat eaters. They follow their prey.

Snow leopards follow their prey, such as mountain goats, down the mountain.

Built for Cold Weather

Snow leopards are well suited for the cold. They have long hair with a thick undercoat of wooly fur. This helps keep them warm.

These big cats use their long, thick tails to stay warm as well. They wrap their tails around their bodies. It is like wearing a fur shawl.

Their long tails are useful in other ways, too. The tails help snow leopards keep their balance. This is important when they jump across rocky areas.

Snow leopards also have large chests and strong lungs. This helps them breathe in the thin mountain air. It lets them get the oxygen they need.

Even the color of snow leopards is helpful. Their light fur blends in well with the snow-covered mountains. Their prey cannot easily see them.

Snow leopards can hide from their prey because they blend in with the snow.

A snow leopard quietly stalks its prey before pouncing on it.

Time to Dine

Snow leopards are able hunters. They mostly eat wild sheep and goats. But they can kill animals three times their size!

Snow leopards also hunt smaller prey. Among these are hares, game birds, and small mammals called marmots.

These big cats may quietly stalk their prey or chase it for a short distance. Then they pounce on their victim. They bite down hard on the prey's neck to kill it.

Snow leopards eat their prey slowly. They cannot eat a whole sheep or goat at once. It takes a snow leopard about two to three days to finish a meal. Each of these hunters kills a big animal about every two weeks.

Mating Season

Snow leopards live alone. But males and females come together for a short time to mate. Their mating season is between January and mid-March. Females are ready to mate at two to three years old. Males begin mating when they are four.

Although snow leopards usually live alone, they are together during mating season.

By May or June, the females give birth. Most times there will be two or three cubs. The cubs are born in a well-hidden, rocky den. It is lined with some of the mother's fur. This helps keep the cubs warm. It gives them a soft place to rest, too.

Snow leopards usually have two or three cubs.

Here Come the Cubs

Snow leopard cubs are born small and helpless. Most only weigh about a pound. They do not even open their eyes for a week after birth. They look a little like kittens.

The young cubs need their mothers for everything. Their fathers are not around. The males leave after mating.

The cubs eat their first solid meal when they are two months old. At three months, they begin going out with their mother. She teaches them to hunt.

A baby snow leopard rests on its mother's fur. It depends on its mother for everything.

The cubs stay with their mothers until they are eighteen to twenty-two months old. By then, they have learned how to live on the mountain. They are ready to be on their own.

Snow leopard cubs stay with their mothers until they can live by themselves on the mountain.

Troubled Times

The world's snow leopards are endangered animals. This means that they are in danger of disappearing from Earth forever. Sadly, humans are a big part of the problem. Some people kill these beautiful cats. They sell their skins to make coats. It takes six to twelve skins to make just one long coat.

The cats' bones are sold, too, and used in folk medicine. They sell for lots of money—about twice as much as the skins.

In some places, farmers have moved further into areas where snow leopards live. They let their animals graze on the mountains. At times, hungry snow leopards have eaten the farmers' animals. In return, angry farmers shoot the big cats. Large numbers of snow leopards have been killed by farmers and hunters. There are now fewer of these animals than ever before.

Snow leopards are endangered, which means they may disappear from Earth forever.

Some people try to help snow leopards. This young worker is part of a group that helps prevent the hunting of snow leopards.

Save Those Cats!

Some groups are trying to save the snow leopards. They do studies and work with businesses and governments. They help people live better with the snow leopards.

Nations are also working together to help. They have passed laws to protect these big cats. It is now a crime to harm or kill them.

Work has been done to save their habitats, too. Some of these places have been turned into national parks. People cannot hunt in these parks. This helps the animals that live there.

There are only between 4,500 and 7,000 snow leopards left in the wild. We need to keep these big cats alive. They are far too rare and beautiful to lose.

Fun Facts About Snow Leopards

❅ Unlike other big cats, these cats do not roar.

❅ Each leopard has its own pattern of spots. It is like a fingerprint. No two patterns are the same.

❅ ‘Snow leopards are the least aggressive of all big cats. There are no known attacks by snow leopards on humans.

❅ A snow leopard often wraps its tail around its face. This protects its nose from frostbite.

❅ These cats can live for about twenty-one years in zoos. No one is sure how long they live in the wild.

❅ There are about six hundred of these cats in zoos today.

Learn More

Books

Catala, Ellen. *Animals in Danger*. Bloomington, Minn.: Yellow Umbrella Books, 2006.

Kalman, Bobbie, and Hadley Dyer. *Endangered Leopards*. New York: Crabtree Books, 2005.

Squire, Ann O. *Leopards*. New York: Children's Press, 2005.

Web Sites

Snow Leopard Conservancy. *Snow Leopards for Kids*. <http://www.snowleopardconservancy.org/kids/text/kidfax.htm>

Snow Leopard Trust. *Cat Facts*. <http://www.snowleopard.org/catfactsclassroom/catfacts>

Index

B

balance, 12
blending in, 12

C

Central Asia, 10
China, 10
cubs, 18, 20
    food, 20
    living alone, 23
    weight, 20

D

den, 18

E

endangered animal, 24

F

farmers, 24
feet, 8
food, 10, 15
fur, 6, 12, 18

G

goats, 10, 15

H

hunting, 15, 20, 24, 27

K

keeping warm, 12, 18

L

living alone, 10, 16, 23
lungs, 12

M

mammals, 15
mating, 16, 20
mating season, 16
mountain, 4, 10, 12, 23, 24

O

oxygen, 12

P

prey, 10, 12, 15

S

skin, 24
snow leopard
    body, 4, 12
    bones, 24
    color, 12
    effect of humans on, 24
    habitat, 4, 10, 27
    leaping ability, 8
    number in wild, 27
    protection of, 27
    size, 6
    speed, 8
    weight, 6, 8

T

tails, 6, 12
Tibet, 4

W

wild sheep, 10, 15
winter, 10

Enslow Elementary, an imprint of Enslow Publishers, Inc.
Enslow Elementary® is a registered trademark of Enslow Publishers, Inc.

Library of Congress Cataloging-in-Publication Data:

Landau, Elaine.
 Snow leopards : hunters of the snow and ice / by Elaine Landau.
    p. cm. — (Animals of the snow and ice)
 Includes bibliographical references and index.
 Summary: "Provides information for young readers about snow leopards, including habitat, eating habits, mating, babies, and conservation"—Provided by publisher.
 ISBN 978-0-7660-3463-1
 1. Snow leopard—Juvenile literature. I. Title.
 QL737.C23L358 2011
 599.75'54—dc22

                              2009006482

Printed in the United States of America

112009 Lake Book Manufacturing, Inc., Melrose Park, IL

10 9 8 7 6 5 4 3 2 1

To Our Readers: We have done our best to make sure all Internet Addresses in this book were active and appropriate when we went to press. However, the author and the publisher have no control over and assume no liability for the material available on those Internet sites or on other Web sites they may link to. Any comments or suggestions can be sent by e-mail to comments@enslow.com or to the address on the back cover.

Cover photo: © Pauline S Mills/iStockphoto.com

Photo credits: Alan Carey/Photo Researchers, Inc., p. 22; © 1999, Artville, LLC, p. 5 (map); © Biosphoto/Klein J.-L. & Hubert M.-L./Peter Arnold Inc., p. 17; © Biosphoto/Ruoso Cyril/Peter Arnold Inc, p. 27; Corbis/Photolibrary, pp. 24–25; The Image Bank/Getty Images, 7; © NHPA/Andy Rouse, p. 5; © Pauline S Mills/iStockphoto.com, p. 1; Raghu S. Chundawat/Peter Arnold Inc., p. 10; Reinhard, H./Peter Arnold Inc., p. 29; Ronald Wittek/Mauritius/Photolibrary, p. 21; Shutterstock, pp. 14, 32; © Studio Carlo Dani/Animals Animals, p. 19; Terry Whittaker/Photo Researchers, Inc., p. 11; © Tim Fitzharris/Minden Pictures, p. 13; Tom & Pat Leeson/Photo Researchers, Inc., pp. 3, 9; WILDLIFE/ Peter Arnold Inc., p. 30.

Enslow Elementary
an imprint of

Enslow Publishers, Inc.
40 Industrial Road
Box 398
Berkeley Heights, NJ 07922
USA

http://www.enslow.com